The Whole Story

Series Devotional Guide
Book Two

All Scripture taken from the Holy Bible, NEW INTERNATIONAL VERSION®, NIV® Copyright © 1973, 1978, 1984, 2011 by Biblica, Inc.® Used by permission. All rights reserved worldwide.

NEW INTERNATIONAL VERSION® and NIV® are registered trademarks of Biblica, Inc. Use of either trademark for the offering of goods or services requires the prior written consent of Biblica US, Inc.

Copyright © 2019 Trinity Church

All rights reserved.

ISBN: 978-1-7005-0319-0

Introduction

The Bible can be an intimidating read. It all starts out well with a story we may be familiar with-the story of Adam and Eve and the creation of the world. But a few chapters later, most of us are wondering what any of this has to do with the story of salvation that is told in the New Testament. How does the Bible all fit together? How do stories that seem so dissimilar tell the whole story of God's plan for the world and his people?

Trinity Church has embarked on a year-long study of *The Whole Story* of the Bible. Each week, the pastors at Trinity will be taking us through stories that define scripture and explaining how they are a part of the bigger picture of salvation that God tells in the Bible. This study guide is a tool that is intended to be used alongside that teaching to help bring those stories to life in your own day-to-day.

With six daily readings and response pages per week, you will have an opportunity to follow along and understand the whole story of the Bible on a personal level. Inside the journal, you will also find tips to take your time with God deeper and to challenge yourself to share what you are learning with others.

It is our prayer that this year you will begin to see *The Whole Story* - and that it would change your story.

Contents

How to Guide	i
Advent: A Unique Perspective	1
Jesus' Earthly Ministry: Year 1	45
Jesus' Earthly Ministry: Year 2	99
Jesus' Earthly Ministry: Year 3	143
The Cross	197
Going Deeper	221
Who We Are	237

How-to Guide

Welcome to your "The Whole Story" series devotional guide. To get started, grab a pen, open your Bible and prepare your heart to spend some time with the Lord.

There are no right or wrong answers – and there is no homework to turn in! Your journey is yours alone, and how much or how little you do in your guide each day is up to you. Being consistent in your study may mean developing a routine. Work on your guide at a favorite coffee shop before work, in your comfy chair in the evening, or maybe at your kitchen table with your cup of coffee. Whenever you start your time each day, pray for the Lord to open your heart and mind to learn and hear from him.

Give yourself room to miss a day or two, but then get back into the pages of your guide. If you miss more than a few days, don't sweat it. Start today and get ready for the upcoming message.

Here's what's in your journal:

- Guide pages for 6 days of the week which complement the weekly messages and will help review characters, themes and topics you are hearing about
- Weekly message note pages at the end of each week
- Community Group notes
- Pages in the back for additional notes such as:
    - Prayers
    - Memory verse record sheet

The Whole Story

- *Family* - At the beginning of each new chapter we have added a family section with ideas and activities that may help you dig deeper into The Whole Story with your family. (See pages 222-224 for additional information on how to include your entire family.)

Here's how the daily guide pages work:

Date -You guessed it. Write the day's date so you can look back at how God moved throughout the year.

Praise - Write down at least one thing you are grateful for each day. And here's a catch- the challenge is "no repeats" for an entire year! That means each day you have a chance to dig deep and consider all that you have to be thankful for.

Reading – The Bible references listed will be the chapter or chapters of the Bible that you're reading that day. This guide will walk you through the "Whole Story" of the Bible in a year. Daily readings will not take you through every word of the Bible but will guide you through the main stories from beginning to end.

Observations - Write down what you noticed in the chapter you read. Maybe start by asking *Who, What, When, Where and Why?* Other observations may come by asking, "Does anything point to Jesus in this reading? How?" You can also write down what resonates with you, what makes you uncomfortable, what the reading has to say about God or mankind, or additional questions you'd like to research or discuss with your Community Group. This section will be different for everyone. The goal is for you to dig deeper into what you are reading.

Key Verse – Write out the one verse that seems to summarize today's reading or that stands out as something that you might want to study more or pray over.

Application - This is where the hard work comes in. You have prayed, read, studied and written. Now the goal is to figure out

How-to Guide

how to apply what you've learned to your life - today! What specific thing is God's Word telling you to do or not do? Sometimes this is so very clear and other times it may take some patience as you read the passage again and reflect and pray about how God is speaking to you.

Prayer – Write out what *you* want to talk about with the Lord. That might be a confession, a plan to make a change, or a request for help getting through what's next. This is personal and between you and the Lord. This is not the place to write out prayer requests for other people - we've included space for that in the last few pages of the journal. Here is where you get detailed and specific with the Lord – about you!

Share - We recommend that you find one or two (no more than two!) people that are also working through the guide and plan to text or email them your key verse every day. You don't even have to be reading the same day or chapter. Just text the verse and a sentence about why that verse stood out to you. Of course, there may be some days your key verse is something you'd prefer not to share. But if you do share, write down the name of the person you shared it with. You never know when you look back how God may have used that verse in your life or theirs!

Going Deeper – With each daily reading we included two questions to help guide your observations and application if you want to dig a little bit deeper.

It is our hope that this study will draw you deeper into fellowship with God through Christ and that you will be excited to share your key verse with someone in your life.

The Whole Story

Weeks One to Four

The Whole Story

Including Your Entire Family in The Whole Story:
(see pages 222-224 for more ideas on including the entire family every day)

ADVENT

Big Truth
God came because He loves you.

Sing
O Come, O Come Emmanuel

Pray
Sing to the LORD a new song,
  for he has done marvelous things;
his right hand and his holy arm
  have worked salvation for him.
The LORD has made his salvation known
  and revealed his righteousness to the nations.
He has remembered his love
  and his faithfulness to Israel;
all the ends of the earth have seen
  the salvation of our God.

Psalm 98:1-3

Read and Talk About
Matthew 1:18-25

Memorize
"The Word became flesh and made his dwelling among us. We have seen his glory, the glory of the one and only Son, who came from the Father, full of grace and truth."   John 1:14

Activity
Light candles during the Family Scripture Celebration. This will set the time apart and set a holiday tone.

The Whole Story

Reading: Isaiah 1   Date: _____

Praise: _____

_____

Observations: _____

_____

_____

_____

_____

_____

_____

_____

Key Verse: _____

_____

How can I apply this? _____

_____

_____

_____

Prayer: _____

_____

_____

_____

Who can I share this with? _____

Going Deeper:
Observe – What was the Lord weary of? What was Israel to do?
Apply – Verses 18-19 offer hope – how will that come?

Advent – A Unique Perspective

Reading: Isaiah 2   Date: _____

Praise: _____
_____

Observations: _____
_____
_____
_____
_____
_____
_____
_____
_____

Key Verse: _____
_____

How can I apply this? _____
_____
_____
_____

Prayer: _____
_____
_____
_____

Who can I share this with? _____

Going Deeper:
O – *Write an outline of what Isaiah saw.*
A – *In verse 5, Isaiah encouraged Israel to do something. What? Why? Explain.*

The Whole Story

Reading: Isaiah 9   Date: _____

Praise: _____

_____

Observations: _____

_____

_____

_____

_____

_____

_____

_____

Key Verse: _____

_____

How can I apply this? _____

_____

_____

_____

Prayer: _____

_____

_____

_____

Who can I share this with? _____

Going Deeper:

O – In verses 6-7, Isaiah gives great hope – summarize what he wrote.

A – What brings you hope today as we start the advent season?

Advent – A Unique Perspective

Reading: Isaiah 40   Date: _____

Praise: _____

_____

Observations: _____

_____

_____

_____

_____

_____

_____

Key Verse: _____

_____

How can I apply this? _____

_____

_____

_____

Prayer: _____

_____

_____

_____

Who can I share this with? _____

Going Deeper:
O – *Write out what the prophet Isaiah heard about the goodness of the Lord.*
A – *Choose one of these and explain how it brings you comfort today.*

The Whole Story

Reading: Isaiah 51   Date: _____

Praise: _____

_____

Observations: _____

_____

_____

_____

_____

_____

_____

_____

Key Verse: _____

_____

How can I apply this? _____

_____

_____

_____

Prayer: _____

_____

_____

_____

Who can I share this with? _____

Going Deeper:

O – The Lord is calling His people to do what? Why?

A – "Listen", "awake", "lift your eyes" – which of these do I need to do most today? Write a short plan.

Advent – A Unique Perspective

Reading: Isaiah 61   Date: _____

Praise: _____
_____

Observations: _____
_____
_____
_____
_____
_____
_____
_____

Key Verse: _____
_____

How can I apply this? _____
_____
_____
_____

Prayer: _____
_____
_____
_____

Who can I share this with? _____

Going Deeper:
O – Isaiah responds to God's promises of hope and restoration in verses 10-11. What did the Lord promise and to whom?
A – Are these promises evident today? Explain.

The Whole Story

Message NotesDate:_____

Advent – A Unique Perspective

Message Notes

The Whole Story

Community Group Notes   Date:_____

Advent – A Unique Perspective

Community Group Notes

The Whole Story

Reading: Isaiah 53   Date: _____

Praise: _____

_____

Observations: _____

_____
_____
_____
_____
_____
_____
_____

Key Verse: _____

_____

How can I apply this? _____

_____
_____
_____

Prayer: _____

_____
_____
_____

Who can I share this with? _____

Going Deeper:
O – In Acts 8:31-33, Philip used verse 7 to share the Good News of Jesus with the eunuch. Where else is this verse referenced or quoted? Why?
A – The first few verses describe how human and like us Jesus would appear on earth. What kind of Messiah was Israel expecting? How does this influence what I believe about Jesus' birth?

Advent – A Unique Perspective

Reading: Ruth 1　　　　　Date: _____

Praise: _____

_____

Observations: _____

_____

_____

_____

_____

_____

_____

Key Verse: _____

_____

How can I apply this? _____

_____

_____

_____

Prayer: _____

_____

_____

_____

Who can I share this with? _____

Going Deeper:

O – Skim through Ruth 4. At the end is a short genealogy that connects Ruth's 2nd husband Boaz to King David. Ruth was from where?

A – Ruth's mother-in-law Naomi showed great faith (explain how). Ruth promised to follow Naomi's God (verses 16-17). What questions do you have about how they fit into the story of Jesus' genealogy?

The Whole Story

Reading: 1 Kings 2   Date: _____

Praise: _____

Observations: _____

_____
_____
_____
_____
_____
_____
_____

Key Verse: _____
_____

How can I apply this? _____
_____
_____
_____

Prayer: _____
_____
_____
_____

Who can I share this with? _____

Going Deeper:

O – Solomon became King of Israel after David died. Who tried to overthrow his kingship? How? Why?

A – David's sons went to great lengths to try to thwart the will of God. Is there something that I know God wants me to do (or not do) that I am fighting against?

Advent – A Unique Perspective

Reading: 2 Chronicles 29   Date: _____

Praise: _____

_____

Observations: _____

_____

_____

_____

_____

_____

_____

_____

Key Verse: _____

_____

How can I apply this? _____

_____

_____

_____

Prayer: _____

_____

_____

_____

Who can I share this with? _____

Going Deeper:
O – *What had happened in temple worship through the generations from Solomon to Hezekiah. What did Hezekiah do?*
A – *Are there parts of my worship/relationship with the Lord that need renewed?*

The Whole Story

Reading: Haggai 1 Date: _____

Praise: _____
_____

Observations: _____
_____
_____
_____
_____
_____
_____
_____

Key Verse: _____
_____

How can I apply this? _____
_____
_____
_____

Prayer: _____
_____
_____
_____

Who can I share this with? _____

Going Deeper:
O – Israel has returned from captivity in Babylon. What does the Lord tell Zerubbabel to do through the prophet Haggai? Why?
A – Is there something in verses 5 and 6 that could apply to my life? What should I do as a response?

Advent – A Unique Perspective

Reading: Matthew 1   Date: _____

Praise: _____

_____

Observations: _____

_____

_____

_____

_____

_____

_____

_____

Key Verse: _____

_____

How can I apply this? _____

_____

_____

_____

Prayer: _____

_____

_____

_____

Who can I share this with? _____

Going Deeper:

O – Make a list of any of the names in Jesus' genealogy that you recognize. Search for one or two that you do not recognize and make some notes about what you discover.

A – Why is this list of names important to The Whole Story? What does it say to me?

The Whole Story

Message Notes   Date:_____

Advent – A Unique Perspective

Message Notes

The Whole Story

Community Group Notes   Date:_____

Community Group Notes

The Whole Story

Reading: Romans 4 & 5   Date: _____

Praise: _____

_____

Observations: _____

_____

_____

_____

_____

_____

_____

_____

Key Verse: _____

_____

How can I apply this? _____

_____

_____

_____

Prayer: _____

_____

_____

_____

Who can I share this with? _____

Going Deeper:

O – Jesus came to the earth for a purpose. What was it? Why was it necessary?

A – Reflect on Romans 5:10. "Saved" from what? "Reconciled" to whom? Is this evident in my life?

Advent – A Unique Perspective

Reading: Acts 7   Date: _____

Praise: _____
_____

Observations: _____
_____
_____
_____
_____
_____
_____
_____

Key Verse: _____
_____

How can I apply this? _____
_____
_____
_____

Prayer: _____
_____
_____
_____

Who can I share this with? _____

Going Deeper:

O – Outline the history that Stephen gave. Is there anything I hadn't known before in his speech? What?

A – Why was the crowd so angry with him? What did Stephen condemn the crowd for? What is my relationship with the Holy Spirit?

The Whole Story

Reading: Hebrews 5 & 6   Date: _____

Praise: _____
_____

Observations: _____
_____
_____
_____
_____
_____
_____
_____

Key Verse: _____
_____

How can I apply this? _____
_____
_____
_____

Prayer: _____
_____
_____
_____

Who can I share this with? _____

Going Deeper:
O – Outline God's covenants and promises and how Jesus fulfilled them.
A – Why was the retelling of these promises and fulfillments so important to Israel then and to me today?

Advent – A Unique Perspective

Reading: Hebrews 7   Date: _____

Praise: _____

_____

Observations: _____

_____
_____
_____
_____
_____
_____
_____

Key Verse: _____

_____

How can I apply this? _____

_____
_____
_____

Prayer: _____

_____
_____
_____

Who can I share this with? _____

Going Deeper:
O – Also read Psalm 110. David was called into the royal priesthood and was not of the priestly lineage of the Levites. Explain how this royal priesthood applies to Jesus.
A – Verses 24-25 explain how Jesus relates to us. Do I have a relationship with Jesus that is lifesaving?

The Whole Story

Reading: Hebrews 8   Date: _____

Praise: _____
_____

Observations: _____
_____
_____
_____
_____
_____
_____
_____

Key Verse: _____
_____

How can I apply this? _____
_____
_____
_____

Prayer: _____
_____
_____
_____

Who can I share this with? _____

Going Deeper:
O – Review Jeremiah 31 for more context. What did Israel not do? What did the Lord promise to do? How does Jesus fit?
A – Reflect on verse 12. Do I believe this applies to me? Why or why not?

Advent – A Unique Perspective

Reading: Luke 1   Date: _____

Praise: _____
_____

Observations: _____
_____
_____
_____
_____
_____
_____
_____
_____

Key Verse: _____
_____

How can I apply this? _____
_____
_____
_____

Prayer: _____
_____
_____
_____

Who can I share this with? _____

Going Deeper:
O – Outline Mary's praise and then Zechariah's. How do they overlap, if at all?
A – Our journey through The Whole Story seems to come to a great crescendo in these few verses. What should my response be?

The Whole Story

Message Notes   Date:_____

Advent – A Unique Perspective

Message Notes

The Whole Story

Community Group Notes   Date:_____

Community Group Notes

The Whole Story

Reading: Colossians 1   Date: _____

Praise: _____

Observations: _____

_____
_____
_____
_____
_____
_____
_____

Key Verse: _____

_____

How can I apply this? _____

_____
_____
_____

Prayer: _____

_____
_____
_____

Who can I share this with? _____

Going Deeper:

O – In Jesus _____ (fill in the blanks, verses 16-17). In verse 18, Paul writes that Jesus is: _____. How and why did God send Jesus to fill the gap between creation and the cross?

A – If Paul were to write about my life today, would it look much like what he wrote to the church in Colossae? Why or why not?

Advent – A Unique Perspective

Reading: Philippians 2 Date: _____

Praise: _____
_____

Observations: _____
_____
_____
_____
_____
_____
_____
_____
_____

Key Verse: _____
_____

How can I apply this? _____
_____
_____
_____

Prayer: _____
_____
_____
_____

Who can I share this with? _____

Going Deeper:
O – Outline verses 6 though 11.
A – Jesus came to earth with the nature of a servant. In verses 3-4, Paul exhorts the church in Philippi to do what? In what ways can I serve others well?

The Whole Story

Reading: Hebrews 2 & 3   Date: _____

Praise: _____

_____

Observations: _____

_____

_____

_____

_____

_____

_____

_____

Key Verse: _____

_____

How can I apply this? _____

_____

_____

_____

_____

Prayer: _____

_____

_____

_____

Who can I share this with? _____

Going Deeper:

O – Make a list of what you learned about Jesus having to come to earth in human form. Why was it necessary? What did He accomplish?

A – How do verses 2:12-14 and 3:14-15 apply to me and my relationship with Jesus?

Advent – A Unique Perspective

Reading: 1 John 4   Date: _____

Praise: _____

_____

Observations: _____

_____

_____

_____

_____

_____

_____

_____

Key Verse: _____

_____

How can I apply this? _____

_____

_____

Prayer: _____

_____

_____

_____

Who can I share this with? _____

Going Deeper:

O – How did God show His love among us? God sent His son to be: _____ (verse 10). John tells us to test spirits that may be from God by what standard? (verses 2-3)

A – "We love because He first loved us" (verse 19). Do I know that love from the Father today? Explain.

The Whole Story

Reading: 1 John 5   Date: _____

Praise: _____

_____

Observations: _____

_____

_____

_____

_____

_____

_____

_____

Key Verse: _____

_____

How can I apply this? _____

_____

_____

_____

Prayer: _____

_____

_____

_____

Who can I share this with? _____

Going Deeper:

O – Verse 5 summarizes the hope of Christmas. Explain.

A – Verse 13 is a summary of our hope in Jesus. Do I have this assurance of eternal life? If you have confessed your belief in the Lord Jesus, know that this promise applies to you. If you recently made this confession, please reach out to your campus pastor or by email to info@trinitychurchvb.com so that we can connect with you.

Advent – A Unique Perspective

Reading: John 1   Date: _____

Praise: _____

_____

Observations: _____

_____

_____

_____

_____

_____

_____

Key Verse: _____

_____

How can I apply this? _____

_____

_____

_____

Prayer: _____

_____

_____

_____

Who can I share this with? _____

Going Deeper:

O – What does "in the world" mean? Why did Jesus, God's Son, come into the world?

A – Reflect on verses 14 and 18 – the one and only son. Why does John identify Jesus this way? Do I identify Jesus this way?

The Whole Story

Message Notes   Date:_____

Message Notes

The Whole Story

Community Group Notes   Date:_____

Advent – A Unique Perspective

Community Group Notes

The Whole Story

Jesus' Earthly Ministry
Year 1

Weeks Five to Nine

The Whole Story

Including Your Entire Family in The Whole Story:

Jesus' Earthly Ministry: Year 1

Big Truth
We can trust God.

Sing
Trust and Obey

Pray
In you, LORD my God,
  I put my trust.
Show me your ways, LORD,
  teach me your paths.
Guide me in your truth and teach me,
  for you are God my Savior,
  and my hope is in you all day long.

Psalm 25:1, 4-5

Read and Talk About
Matthew 4:18-22

Memorize
But seek first his kingdom and his righteousness, and all these things will be given to you as well. Therefore, do not worry about tomorrow, for tomorrow will worry about itself. Each day has enough trouble of its own.   Matthew 6:33-34

Activity
In advance, choose a good thing to have waiting in a different room, like a plate of cookies. Without explanation, tell your family to follow. Lead them in a roundabout way to the good thing. Talk about how Jesus' disciples followed without question, without skepticism, without any assurance of what awaited them. Ask why the disciples may have followed in that way.

The Whole Story

Reading: Matthew 2   Date: _____

Praise: _____

_____

Observations: _____

_____
_____
_____
_____
_____
_____
_____

Key Verse: _____

_____

How can I apply this? _____

_____
_____
_____

Prayer: _____

_____
_____
_____

Who can I share this with? _____

Going Deeper:
O – Summarize the three stories of Jesus' early life and the prophecies that were fulfilled.
A – Reflect on how Jesus' birth has changed your life.

Jesus' Earthly Ministry: Year 1

Reading: Luke 2 Date: _____

Praise: _____

_____

Observations: _____

_____

_____

_____

_____

_____

_____

_____

Key Verse: _____

_____

How can I apply this? _____

_____

_____

_____

Prayer: _____

_____

_____

_____

Who can I share this with? _____

Going Deeper:
O – Shepherd, angels, wisemen – so many people were amazed at seeing Jesus as an infant and young child. Outline the reactions of those who saw Him including Simeon and Anna.
A – Celebrate the birth of Jesus today. Maybe like the angels by singing or the shepherds telling everyone they saw. Let the glory of His birth surround you and fill you with joy.

The Whole Story

Reading: Matthew 3   Date: _____

Praise: _____
_____

Observations: _____
_____
_____
_____
_____
_____
_____

Key Verse: _____
_____

How can I apply this? _____
_____
_____
_____

Prayer: _____
_____
_____
_____

Who can I share this with? _____

Going Deeper:

O – John the Baptist had a specific purpose for his life. What was it? What was unique about the baptism of Jesus?

A – Do I have a purpose like John the Baptist's that is very clear? If so, what is it? If not, what does it seem to be? Why?

Jesus' Earthly Ministry: Year 1

Reading: John 2 & 3   Date: _____

Praise: _____

_____

Observations: _____

_____

_____

_____

_____

_____

_____

Key Verse: _____

_____

How can I apply this? _____

_____

_____

_____

Prayer: _____

_____

_____

_____

Who can I share this with? _____

Going Deeper:

O – Jesus attended a wedding party and the host ran out of wine. Write the narrative of the story in your own words. What questions do you have about what happened?

A – Nicodemus got a personal lesson on faith and belief. What stands out to you in all that Jesus said to him? How should you respond?

The Whole Story

Reading: Matthew 22   Date: _____

Praise: _____

_____

Observations: _____

_____

_____

_____

_____

_____

_____

_____

Key Verse: _____

_____

How can I apply this? _____

_____

_____

_____

Prayer: _____

_____

_____

_____

Who can I share this with? _____

Going Deeper:

O – The opening of this chapter gives details about a wedding. Make notes on everything that you learned about the customs of the banquet.

A – How is this different from your wedding or to a wedding you have attended? Reflect on a wedding banquet filled with people you don't know. What is the purpose of the wedding banquet?

Jesus' Earthly Ministry: Year 1

Reading: Revelation 19   Date: _____

Praise: _____

_____

Observations: _____

_____

_____

_____

_____

_____

_____

_____

Key Verse: _____

_____

How can I apply this? _____

_____

_____

_____

Prayer: _____

_____

_____

_____

Who can I share this with? _____

Going Deeper:

O – Another look at a wedding banquet – what is the purpose of this banquet? Who is invited? How is this different from the wedding in Matthew 22?

A – Does the thought of attending this wedding banquet give you hope? In what way? Write a short thank you note to the groom for inviting you.

The Whole Story

Message Notes Date:_____

Jesus' Earthly Ministry: Year 1

Message Notes

The Whole Story

Community Group Notes   Date:_____

Jesus' Earthly Ministry: Year 1

Community Group Notes

The Whole Story

Reading: Matthew 4　　　Date: _____

Praise: _____

Observations: _____
_____
_____
_____
_____
_____
_____

Key Verse: _____
_____

How can I apply this? _____
_____
_____
_____

Prayer: _____
_____
_____
_____

Who can I share this with? _____

Going Deeper:
O – Jesus' words in this chapter are brief and to the point. Which are especially meaningful for you today? Why?
A – What do you learn from Jesus' responses to Satan's temptations? How can you use His example to prepare for Satan's next campaign against YOU??

Jesus' Earthly Ministry: Year 1

Reading: Matthew 9   Date: _____

Praise:_____

_____

Observations: _____

_____

_____

_____

_____

_____

_____

_____

Key Verse: _____

_____

How can I apply this? _____

_____

_____

_____

Prayer: _____

_____

_____

_____

Who can I share this with? _____

Going Deeper:

O – Jesus interacts with many individuals and groups in this chapter. Choose one encounter and list the main players along with their responses.

A – Think about a time YOU have encountered Jesus (...in His Word? ...in a sermon?? ...through a specific experience??) What has been your response?

The Whole Story

Reading: Mark 1   Date: _____

Praise: _____
_____

Observations: _____
_____
_____
_____
_____
_____
_____
_____

Key Verse: _____
_____

How can I apply this? _____
_____
_____
_____

Prayer: _____
_____
_____
_____

Who can I share this with? _____

Going Deeper:
O – List four things that happened on that busy Sabbath in Capernaum. What did Jesus do the very next morning?
A – Jesus made it a habit to speak alone with His Father first thing in the morning. How could/does this habit impact your life?

Jesus' Earthly Ministry: Year 1

Reading: Luke 4   Date: _____

Praise: _____

_____

Observations: _____

_____

_____

_____

_____

_____

_____

_____

_____

Key Verse: _____

_____

How can I apply this? _____

_____

_____

_____

Prayer: _____

_____

_____

_____

Who can I share this with? _____

Going Deeper:

O – Why were the people at the synagogue in Nazareth so angry with Jesus that they wanted to throw Him off the cliff?

A – Have you ever been offended by anything Jesus said? What did you do about it?

The Whole Story

Reading: Luke 5   Date: _____

Praise: _____

_____

Observations: _____

_____
_____
_____
_____
_____
_____
_____

Key Verse: _____

_____

How can I apply this? _____

_____
_____
_____

Prayer: _____

_____
_____
_____

Who can I share this with? _____

Going Deeper:
O – Put yourself in Simon's (Peter's) place. What do you think he was thinking/feeling in:
 1) verse 4-5;   2) verses 6-7;   3) verse 8;   4) verses 10-11
A – This story tracks what drew Peter to follow Jesus. What is drawing/drew YOU to follow Jesus?

Jesus' Earthly Ministry: Year 1

Reading: Malachi 4   Date: _____

Praise: _____

_____

Observations: _____

_____

_____

_____

_____

_____

_____

_____

Key Verse: _____

_____

How can I apply this? _____

_____

_____

Prayer: _____

_____

_____

_____

Who can I share this with? _____

Going Deeper:

O – What 'day' is referred to in this passage? What is the difference between the two groups of people mentioned and their experience on this 'day'? Why do you think we are reading it at this point in our study?

A – To which group do you belong? How do you know?

The Whole Story

Message Notes   Date:_____

Jesus' Earthly Ministry: Year 1

Message Notes

The Whole Story

Community Group Notes   Date:_____

Jesus' Earthly Ministry: Year 1

Community Group Notes

The Whole Story

Reading: Matthew 6   Date: _____

Praise: _____

_____

Observations: _____

_____

_____

_____

_____

_____

_____

_____

Key Verse: _____

_____

How can I apply this? _____

_____

_____

_____

Prayer: _____

_____

_____

_____

Who can I share this with? _____

Going Deeper:
O – As part of His Sermon on the Mount, Jesus gives very specific instructions to His followers regarding worrying. Read verses 25-34 several times and then summarize the passage.
A – Write a short prayer about one thing that you have worried about recently. Tell God all about your worry. And then leave that worry right on this page – knowing that God has heard your prayer.

Jesus' Earthly Ministry: Year 1

Reading: Psalm 23   Date: _____

Praise:_____

_____

Observations: _____

_____

_____

_____

_____

_____

_____

_____

Key Verse: _____

_____

How can I apply this? _____

_____

_____

_____

Prayer: _____

_____

_____

_____

Who can I share this with? _____

Going Deeper:

O – Read Psalm 23 in at least two other translations. Write it out in your own words.

A – Once you have written Psalm 23 down, read it out loud as a prayer back to the Lord. (example: Thank you Lord that you are my shepherd....). What phrase or verse stands out? Why?

The Whole Story

Reading: Psalm 27   Date: _____

Praise: _____
_____

Observations: _____
_____
_____
_____
_____
_____
_____
_____

Key Verse: _____
_____

How can I apply this? _____
_____
_____
_____

Prayer: _____
_____
_____
_____

Who can I share this with? _____

Going Deeper:

O – The author asks boldly for what from the Lord? What is he certain of? Who will care for him? What is his final affirmation to the reader?

A – How does this psalm bring you comfort today? How does the word "wait" encourage or discourage you today? (Read on to Psalm 28 if today is a day where you need more encouragement).

Jesus' Earthly Ministry: Year 1

Reading: Philippians 4   Date: _____

Praise: _____

_____

Observations: _____

_____
_____
_____
_____
_____
_____
_____

Key Verse: _____

_____

How can I apply this? _____

_____
_____
_____

Prayer: _____

_____
_____
_____

Who can I share this with? _____

Going Deeper:

O – Write out verses 6 and 7. Paul is writing to the church in Philippi and closes his letter with a similar assurance of God's goodness in verses 19-20. How did the chapter start in verse 1? What one word sums up how Paul might have been feeling?

A – What does Paul tell the church to focus on in verses 8-9? How can I reflect God's peace in my life today?

The Whole Story

Reading: Psalm 107   Date: _____

Praise: _____
_____

Observations: _____
_____
_____
_____
_____
_____
_____
_____

Key Verse: _____
_____

How can I apply this? _____
_____
_____
_____

Prayer: _____
_____
_____
_____

Who can I share this with? _____

Going Deeper:
O – In verses 4, 10, 17 and 23 there are 4 different groups of peoples. Make a list of their issues, what they did (this is the same for all 4), and the results.
A – Do I need to reach out the way the people in this Psalm did? Go ahead! Write out your plea and ask the Lord for what you need.

Jesus' Earthly Ministry: Year 1

Reading: Proverbs 3   Date: _____

Praise: _____

_____

Observations: _____

_____

_____

_____

_____

_____

_____

_____

Key Verse: _____

_____

How can I apply this? _____

_____

_____

_____

Prayer: _____

_____

_____

_____

Who can I share this with? _____

Going Deeper:

O – Read through the passage in more than one translation. Briefly summarize each sentence in verses 1-12. What stands out the most?
A – Verse 5 is often quoted. What does it mean to you? Summarize it and pray it back to the Lord. How can you live today like this is your life verse?

The Whole Story

Message Notes   Date:_____

Jesus' Earthly Ministry: Year 1

Message Notes

The Whole Story

Community Group Notes   Date:_____

Jesus' Earthly Ministry: Year 1

Community Group Notes

The Whole Story

Reading: Mark 4 Date: _____

Praise: _____

_____

Observations: _____

_____

_____

_____

_____

_____

_____

_____

Key Verse: _____

_____

How can I apply this? _____

_____

_____

_____

Prayer: _____

_____

_____

_____

Who can I share this with? _____

Going Deeper:

O – Take short notes about each of the 4 parables and the story of calming the storm. Why did Jesus teach in parables? Which different types of people was He teaching?

A – In verse 40 the disciples who were in the boat during the storm were questioned by Jesus about their faith. If He asked you that question today – how would you respond? Why?

Jesus' Earthly Ministry: Year 1

Reading: Mark 5　　　　　Date: _____

Praise: _____

_____

Observations: _____

_____

_____

_____

_____

_____

_____

Key Verse: _____

_____

How can I apply this? _____

_____

_____

Prayer: _____

_____

_____

_____

Who can I share this with? _____

Going Deeper:
O – Legion, a woman in the crowd and a synagogue leader's daughter were all healed by Jesus. Make notes on what happened. What is the common thread amongst those who sought healing?
A – True or False (and then explain): The faith that these people had is easy for me to identify with today. My faith is just as strong.

The Whole Story

Reading: Mark 6   Date: _____

Praise: _____
_____

Observations: _____
_____
_____
_____
_____
_____
_____
_____

Key Verse: _____
_____

How can I apply this? _____
_____
_____
_____

Prayer: _____
_____
_____
_____

Who can I share this with? _____

Going Deeper:

O – In verses 53-56, people are starting to recognize Jesus because of the miracles that He and His disciples have been doing. Yet, His disciples were still having trouble with belief. Briefly outline the stories of the hungry crowd and the fear in the boat.

A – How does reading Mark 6 encourage you today? Why? What should my response be?

Jesus' Earthly Ministry: Year 1

Reading: Mark 7   Date: _____

Praise: _____
_____

Observations: _____
_____
_____
_____
_____
_____
_____
_____

Key Verse: _____
_____

How can I apply this? _____
_____
_____
_____

Prayer: _____
_____
_____
_____

Who can I share this with? _____

Going Deeper:
O – In verse 8, Jesus said to the Pharisees, "You have let go of the commands of God and are holding on to human traditions." How does this statement relate to the rest of what He told them in in verses 9-23?
A – Ask God to show you any human traditions that you need to let go of so that you can replace them with God's commands.

The Whole Story

Reading: John 4   Date: _____

Praise: _____
_____

Observations: _____
_____
_____
_____
_____
_____
_____

Key Verse: _____
_____

How can I apply this? _____
_____
_____
_____

Prayer: _____
_____
_____
_____

Who can I share this with? _____

Going Deeper:
O Write out what happened in the story of the Samaritan woman. What was the result of Jesus' intervention in her life?
A – The Samaritans confessed who Jesus was and the royal official in Capernaum had great faith. People were having a hard time keeping quiet about what Jesus was doing. Who have I shared Jesus with this week?

Jesus' Earthly Ministry: Year 1

Reading: Luke 17 	 Date: _____

Praise: _____

_____

Observations: _____

_____

_____

_____

_____

_____

_____

_____

Key Verse: _____

_____

How can I apply this? _____

_____

_____

_____

Prayer: _____

_____

_____

_____

Who can I share this with? _____

Going Deeper:
O – Another Samaritan was healed (verses 11-19). What was the man's response? How many were healed with him? Summarize.
A – The Samaritans were outside of the chosen people of God, yet many believed. Contrast the Samaritans with the people in Jesus' hometown (see John 4:44, Luke 4:24, 28-29). How might familiarity with Jesus affect my faith today?

The Whole Story

Message Notes   Date:_____

Jesus' Earthly Ministry: Year 1

Message Notes

The Whole Story

Community Group Notes   Date:_____

Jesus' Earthly Ministry: Year 1

Community Group Notes

The Whole Story

Reading: Matthew 8   Date: _____

Praise: _____

_____

Observations: _____

_____
_____
_____
_____
_____
_____
_____

Key Verse: _____

_____

How can I apply this? _____

_____
_____
_____

Prayer: _____

_____
_____
_____

Who can I share this with? _____

Going Deeper:
O – Write out the key points in these three healings. What is the common theme?
A – Which requires greater faith (if either)? – Asking with faith to be healed OR waiting expectantly for Jesus to answer your prayer? Explain.

Jesus' Earthly Ministry: Year 1

Reading: Matthew 14   Date: _____

Praise: _____

_____

Observations: _____

_____
_____
_____
_____
_____
_____
_____

Key Verse: _____

_____

How can I apply this? _____

_____
_____
_____

Prayer: _____

_____
_____
_____

Who can I share this with? _____

Going Deeper:

O – Two great miracles of Jesus are included in this chapter. Write out what was needed, who was involved, what they said, why – and how Jesus responded.

A – Again we see Jesus being Lord over whatever dilemma the disciples faced. How does His steady response comfort you today?

The Whole Story

Reading: Matthew 15   Date: _____

Praise: _____

_____

Observations: _____

_____

_____

_____

_____

_____

_____

_____

Key Verse: _____

_____

How can I apply this? _____

_____

_____

_____

Prayer: _____

_____

_____

_____

Who can I share this with? _____

Going Deeper:

O – We've seen the story of the mother asking for her daughter to be healed before (in Mark 7). It is followed here in verses 29-31 with a glimpse of how the crowds responded. To whom did they give Glory? Why?

A – How do you respond when God answers a prayer? Is there a Glory report that you need to give to the Lord today?

Jesus' Earthly Ministry: Year 1

Reading: Mark 8   Date: _____

Praise: _____

_____

Observations: _____

_____

_____

_____

_____

_____

_____

Key Verse: _____

_____

How can I apply this? _____

_____

_____

Prayer: _____

_____

_____

Who can I share this with? _____

Going Deeper:
O – In Matthew 15 and here, we see Jesus feeding a large group with a few fish and some bread. What happened? How? Why? Is there anything different between the two accounts?
A – Can put yourself in the midst of the disciples on that day? What questions might you have had for Jesus when He first told them what to do? After everyone was fed?

The Whole Story

Reading: Luke 7   Date: _____

Praise: _____

_____

Observations: _____

_____

_____

_____

_____

_____

_____

_____

Key Verse: _____

_____

How can I apply this? _____

_____

_____

_____

Prayer: _____

_____

_____

_____

Who can I share this with? _____

Going Deeper:

O – Is there anything different in Luke's account from Matthew's? The Centurion demonstrated _____ when he approached Jesus. In the next story, we see a woman's son being raised from the dead – what was the crowd's reaction? What is different?

A – "For we walk by faith, not by sight." (2 Cor 5:7). Is there a place in your life that you need to walk more by faith? Discuss with the Lord.

Jesus' Earthly Ministry: Year 1

Reading: John 6   Date: _____

Praise: _____

_____

Observations: _____

_____

_____

_____

_____

_____

_____

_____

Key Verse: _____

_____

How can I apply this? _____

_____

_____

_____

Prayer: _____

_____

_____

_____

Who can I share this with? _____

Going Deeper:

O – Starting in verse 26, Jesus challenges the crowd about why they are looking for Him. Summarize verses 26-59. Highlight anything that is not clear.

A – The issue for everyone who follows Jesus is the eternal choice that we each have to make. Where are you in your faith journey? Ask the Lord to show you any next steps that you need to take.

The Whole Story

Message Notes   Date:_____

Message Notes

The Whole Story

Community Group Notes   Date:_____

Jesus' Earthly Ministry: Year 1

Community Group Notes

The Whole Story

Jesus' Earthly Ministry
Year 2

Weeks Ten to Thirteen

The Whole Story

Including Your Entire Family in The Whole Story:

Jesus' Earthly Ministry: Year 2

Big Truth
Jesus has compassion on me.

Sing
What a Friend We Have in Jesus

Pray
One thing I ask from the Lord,
  this only do I seek:
that I may dwell in the house of the Lord
  all the days of my life,

to gaze on the beauty of the Lord
  and to seek him in his temple.

Psalm 27:4

Read and Talk About
Matthew 20:20-34

Memorize
Jesus had compassion on them and touched their eyes. Immediately they received their sight and followed him.

Matthew 20:34

Activity
Put every family member's name on a slip of paper. Put the slips in a bowl and have everyone draw a name, making sure no one draws himself. Each person needs to think of an act of service to perform for the person on their slip. Talk about what serving your family means.

The Whole Story

Reading: John 7　　　　　Date: _____

Praise: _____

_____

Observations: _____

_____

_____

_____

_____

_____

_____

Key Verse: _____

_____

How can I apply this? _____

_____

_____

_____

Prayer: _____

_____

_____

_____

Who can I share this with? _____

Going Deeper:

O – Write out verse 5. Does that seem shocking? Why or why not? In verses 37-38, Jesus gives the solution. Outline what happened and what He said in between these passages.

A – The pharisees are trying to trap Jesus with their legalistic interpretation of the law. Write out a short note about Jesus to the pharisees to try and convince them of the faith that you have.

Jesus' Earthly Ministry: Year 2

Reading: John 8   Date: _____

Praise: _____

_____

Observations: _____

_____
_____
_____
_____
_____
_____
_____

Key Verse: _____

_____

How can I apply this? _____

_____
_____
_____

Prayer: _____

_____
_____
_____

Who can I share this with? _____

Going Deeper:

O – In verse 2-11 there is record of an amazing interaction between Jesus and a woman who, in her culture, was doomed to die by stoning because of her choices. Jesus continues to speak to the pharisees afterwards. Summarize what he said to them (vss 12-20). A – Which statement in verses 12-20 brings you the most comfort? Why? Explain.

The Whole Story

Reading: John 9   Date: _____

Praise: _____

_____

Observations: _____

_____

_____

_____

_____

_____

_____

_____

Key Verse: _____

_____

How can I apply this? _____

_____

_____

_____

Prayer: _____

_____

_____

_____

Who can I share this with? _____

Going Deeper:

O – Summarize in a short paragraph the events and teaching in this chapter.

A – Jesus identifies Himself to the man He healed in verses 35-37. What was the man's response? Have you had a life-changing, belief encouraging experience with Jesus? Give Him thanks today or ask Him for what you need.

Jesus' Earthly Ministry: Year 2

Reading: John 10   Date: _____

Praise: _____

_____

Observations: _____

_____
_____
_____
_____
_____
_____
_____

Key Verse: _____

_____

How can I apply this? _____

_____
_____
_____

Prayer: _____

_____
_____
_____

Who can I share this with? _____

Going Deeper:

O – Sort out what Jesus says about being a shepherd in this chapter by making short lists of what He said about sheep, shepherds, gates, pens, flocks, listening...

A – Who does Jesus say are His sheep? What defines them? How can I be more sheep-like today?

The Whole Story

Reading: Romans 2   Date: _____

Praise: _____

_____

Observations: _____

_____
_____
_____
_____
_____
_____
_____

Key Verse: _____

_____

How can I apply this? _____

_____
_____
_____

Prayer: _____

_____
_____
_____

Who can I share this with? _____

Going Deeper:
O – In John 8, we read about an adulteress and Jesus' response to her. Write an explanation of what Paul is saying to someone who might not be a Jesus follower. (Go back and listen online to the last sermon in the Law mini-series from October 6th as a refresher).
A – Identify one thing that stood out to you today.

Jesus' Earthly Ministry: Year 2

Reading: Leviticus 20   Date: _____

Praise: _____

_____

Observations: _____

_____

_____

_____

_____

_____

_____

Key Verse: _____

_____

How can I apply this? _____

_____

_____

Prayer: _____

_____

_____

_____

Who can I share this with? _____

Going Deeper:
O – Maybe not a chapter to read out loud to young children. The focus this week is on the story at the beginning of John 8. What was most likely going to be the penalty for the woman that Jesus forgave? Why?
A – What does God wants His people to do? Is that hard to do? Explain.

The Whole Story

Message Notes   Date:_____

Jesus' Earthly Ministry: Year 2

Message Notes

The Whole Story

Community Group Notes   Date:_____

Jesus' Earthly Ministry: Year 2

Community Group Notes

The Whole Story

Reading: Matthew 12   Date: _____

Praise: _____
_____

Observations: _____
_____
_____
_____
_____
_____
_____
_____

Key Verse: _____
_____

How can I apply this? _____
_____
_____
_____

Prayer: _____
_____
_____
_____

Who can I share this with? _____

Going Deeper:
O – Outline all that Jesus did – and what He said about the Sabbath.
A – Explain how you keep a Sabbath day – why is it important?
After reading this, what might you want to change, if anything?

Jesus' Earthly Ministry: Year 2

Reading: Matthew 13   Date: _____

Praise:_____

_____

Observations: _____

_____

_____

_____

_____

_____

_____

_____

Key Verse: _____

_____

How can I apply this? _____

_____

_____

_____

Prayer: _____

_____

_____

_____

Who can I share this with? _____

Going Deeper:
O – Much of this chapter was also recorded by Mark in Mark 4. Review Mark 4 from week 8 and note any major differences. Outline the three healings in verses 26-56.
A – Which of these three healings stands out the most? Why?

The Whole Story

Reading: Mark 2 & 3   Date: _____

Praise: _____
_____

Observations: _____
_____
_____
_____
_____
_____
_____
_____

Key Verse: _____
_____

How can I apply this? _____
_____
_____
_____

Prayer: _____
_____
_____
_____

Who can I share this with? _____

Going Deeper:
O – Today's reading is similar to Matthew's account of the same stories in Mathew 12. What is different?
A – What does Jesus say in verses 27-28? Evaluate what we've learned about the Sabbath and explain how these verses apply to us.

Jesus' Earthly Ministry: Year 2

Reading: Luke 13   Date: _____

Praise: _____

_____

Observations: _____

_____
_____
_____
_____
_____
_____
_____

Key Verse: _____

_____

How can I apply this? _____

_____
_____
_____

Prayer: _____

_____
_____
_____

Who can I share this with? _____

Going Deeper:
O – Again Jesus heals on the Sabbath. What was the synagogue leader's response? How did Jesus respond? The crowd?
A – Jesus told a parable about the narrow door/the narrow way. What should my response be?

The Whole Story

Reading: Luke 14   Date: _____

Praise: _____
_____

Observations: _____
_____
_____
_____
_____
_____
_____
_____

Key Verse: _____
_____

How can I apply this? _____
_____
_____
_____

Prayer: _____
_____
_____
_____

Who can I share this with? _____

Going Deeper:
O – Jesus is again confronted about healing on the Sabbath. He follows this with stories about banquets, seating and accepting invitations to attend (or making excuses). Summarize the parables in verses 7-23.
A – Identify yourself as one of the banquet guests or invitees. How should you respond?

Jesus' Earthly Ministry: Year 2

Reading: John 5   Date: _____

Praise: _____

_____

Observations: _____

_____

_____

_____

_____

_____

_____

_____

Key Verse: _____

_____

How can I apply this? _____

_____

_____

_____

Prayer: _____

_____

_____

_____

Who can I share this with? _____

Going Deeper:

O – Jesus heals a man by the pool called Bethesda (on the Sabbath). Write out the questions that Jesus asked the man; the questions others asked the man; and the man's responses. Which question/answer stands out the most? Why?

A – Read verse 24 in more than one translation and write out one of them. Is this verse reassuring? Why?

The Whole Story

Message Notes					Date:_____

Jesus' Earthly Ministry: Year 2

Message Notes

The Whole Story

Community Group Notes   Date:_____

Jesus' Earthly Ministry: Year 2

Community Group Notes

The Whole Story

Reading: Matthew 16   Date: _____

Praise: _____

_____

Observations: _____

_____

_____

_____

_____

_____

_____

Key Verse: _____

_____

How can I apply this? _____

_____

_____

_____

Prayer: _____

_____

_____

_____

Who can I share this with? _____

Going Deeper:
O – Verses 24 – 26 are quite a challenge to one who follows Jesus. Write a short paragraph of introduction to someone you don't know about how your life demonstrates that you are following Jesus.
A – Reflect on what you wrote (or had trouble writing) above.

Jesus' Earthly Ministry: Year 2

Reading: Matthew 19   Date: _____

Praise: _____

_____

Observations: _____

_____

_____

_____

_____

_____

_____

_____

Key Verse: _____

_____

How can I apply this? _____

_____

_____

_____

Prayer: _____

_____

_____

_____

Who can I share this with? _____

Going Deeper:

O – Jesus asks the rich man to do what? Why could that have been difficult? Explain what Jesus was teaching in one or two short sentences.

A – Is there anything that I need to let go of in order to follow Jesus? Explain.

The Whole Story

Reading: Matthew 20   Date: _____

Praise: _____
_____

Observations: _____
_____
_____
_____
_____
_____
_____
_____

Key Verse: _____
_____

How can I apply this? _____
_____
_____
_____

Prayer: _____
_____
_____
_____

Who can I share this with? _____

Going Deeper:
O – The parable of the vineyard workers ends with: "So the last will be first, and the first will be last." Write a paragraph about what Jesus meant to someone who may not have heard this story before. A – In verses 24-28 Jesus teaches about being a servant. How does your life reflect being a servant?

Jesus' Earthly Ministry: Year 2

Reading: Mark 10   Date: _____

Praise: _____

_____

Observations: _____

_____

_____

_____

_____

_____

_____

Key Verse: _____

_____

How can I apply this? _____

_____

_____

Prayer: _____

_____

_____

Who can I share this with? _____
Going Deeper:
O – Mark 10 is a synoptic view of Matthew 19 - 20. Which parables/teachings are the same? Which are different?
A – In Mark 10:51 Jesus asks the blind man a very direct question. If Jesus were to ask you that question today, how would you respond?

The Whole Story

Reading: Luke 18   Date: _____

Praise: _____
_____

Observations: _____
_____
_____
_____
_____
_____
_____
_____

Key Verse: _____
_____

How can I apply this? _____
_____
_____
_____

Prayer: _____
_____
_____
_____

Who can I share this with? _____

Going Deeper:
O – Luke also recounts the stories in Mark 10 and Matthew 19-20. Does anything stand out as different in Luke's account?
A – "Receive the kingdom of God like a child" – what does this mean? Is my response to God's call like that of a child? Why or why not? Explain.

Jesus' Earthly Ministry: Year 2

Reading: John 13   Date: _____

Praise: _____

_____

Observations: _____

_____
_____
_____
_____
_____
_____
_____

Key Verse: _____

_____

How can I apply this? _____

_____
_____
_____

Prayer: _____

_____
_____
_____

Who can I share this with? _____

Going Deeper:
O – Foot washing as an example of servanthood. Explain why this would have been such a visual example in the context where Jesus modelled it. What might be a model of such servanthood today?
A – Our focus this week has been on Jesus' teaching on servanthood. Why did Jesus teach so much on this topic? Why does it matter to His followers? To those who don't yet follow Him?

The Whole Story

Message Notes   Date:_____

Jesus' Earthly Ministry: Year 2

Message Notes

Community Group Notes   Date:_____

Jesus' Earthly Ministry: Year 2

Community Group Notes

The Whole Story

Reading: Matthew 17   Date: _____

Praise: _____

_____

Observations: _____

_____

_____

_____

_____

_____

_____

Key Verse: _____

_____

How can I apply this? _____

_____

_____

_____

Prayer: _____

_____

_____

_____

Who can I share this with? _____

Going Deeper:
O – Why did Jesus send Peter out fishing?
A – Consider one of the following:
    How does this story inform your feelings about the taxes you are required to pay?
    When have you seen Jesus provide miraculously for your needs or the needs of someone you know?

Jesus' Earthly Ministry: Year 2

Reading: Matthew 18   Date: _____

Praise: _____

_____

Observations: _____

_____
_____
_____
_____
_____
_____
_____

Key Verse: _____

_____

How can I apply this? _____

_____
_____
_____

Prayer: _____

_____
_____
_____

Who can I share this with? _____

Going Deeper:

O – Of the five encounters/parables in this chapter, which do you find the most challenging? Which provides you personally with comfort/instruction?

A – Ask God to help you understand the challenging one and watch for His answer. Thank God for the comfort/instruction He provided through this passage and memorize the verse which was most meaningful to you.

The Whole Story

Reading: Mark 9   Date: _____

Praise: _____
_____

Observations: _____
_____
_____
_____
_____
_____
_____
_____

Key Verse: _____
_____

How can I apply this? _____
_____
_____
_____

Prayer: _____
_____
_____
_____

Who can I share this with? _____

Going Deeper:
O – Describe how Jesus LOOKED and ACTED at the time of the Transfiguration.
A – How does this event cause you to see His divinity? What words will you use to describe Him as you worship Him in that capacity?

Jesus' Earthly Ministry: Year 2

Reading: 1 Kings 8   Date: _____

Praise: _____

Observations: _____
_____
_____
_____
_____
_____
_____
_____

Key Verse: _____

How can I apply this? _____
_____
_____

Prayer: _____
_____
_____

Who can I share this with? _____

Going Deeper:
O – How did God dwell with His people in the time of Solomon? What was the proof of His presence?
A – How does God dwell with His people in our time? What is the proof of His presence?

The Whole Story

Reading: Luke 9   Date: _____

Praise: _____
_____

Observations: _____
_____
_____
_____
_____
_____
_____
_____

Key Verse: _____

How can I apply this? _____
_____
_____
_____

Prayer: _____
_____
_____
_____

Who can I share this with? _____

Going Deeper:
O – Compare the three accounts of the Transfiguration we have studied this week. List details which are unique to each account.
A – How does comparing different people's versions of the same event contribute to your understanding of their validity.

Jesus' Earthly Ministry: Year 2

Reading: Psalm 139   Date: _____

Praise: _____
_____

Observations: _____
_____
_____
_____
_____
_____
_____
_____

Key Verse: _____
_____

How can I apply this? _____
_____
_____
_____

Prayer: _____
_____
_____
_____

Who can I share this with? _____

Going Deeper:
O – Reread Psalm 139 as your own prayer of praise and thanksgiving to the Lord, considering the words carefully as coming from your own heart.
A – Which part has the most personal significance for you today? Why?

The Whole Story

Message Notes   Date:_____

Jesus' Earthly Ministry: Year 2

Message Notes

The Whole Story

Community Group Notes   Date:_____

Jesus' Earthly Ministry: Year 2

Community Group Notes

The Whole Story

Jesus' Earthly Ministry
Year 3

Weeks Fourteen to Eighteen

The Whole Story

Including Your Entire Family in The Whole Story:

Jesus' Earthly Ministry: Year 3

Big Truth
Jesus has real power.

Sing
To God Be the Glory

Pray
Create in me a pure heart, O God,
 and renew a steadfast spirit within me.
Do not cast me from your presence
 or take your Holy Spirit from me.
Restore to me the joy of your salvation
 and grant me a willing spirit, to sustain me.

Psalm 51:10-12

Read and Talk About
John 11:38-44

Memorize
John 11:25-26

Activity
Wrap one of your family members to look like a mummy using toilet paper or rags. As goofy as it is, the mental picture will stick when you read about Lazarus coming out from the grave still dressed in his graveclothes.

The Whole Story

Reading: Luke 10   Date: _____

Praise: _____
_____

Observations: _____
_____
_____
_____
_____
_____
_____

Key Verse: _____
_____

How can I apply this? _____
_____
_____
_____

Prayer: _____
_____
_____
_____

Who can I share this with? _____

Going Deeper:

O – Summarize what you read in verses 1-23.

A – Jesus told the 72 upon their return, "Do not rejoice that the spirits submit to you, but rejoice that your names are written in heaven," (verse 20). Rejoice with the 72 for the gift of your salvation.

Jesus' Earthly Ministry: Year 3

Reading: Luke 11 Date: _____

Praise: _____

_____

Observations: _____

_____
_____
_____
_____
_____
_____
_____

Key Verse: _____

_____

How can I apply this? _____

_____
_____
_____

Prayer: _____

_____
_____
_____

Who can I share this with? _____

Going Deeper:

O – Focus on verses 29-32. Also review Matthew 12:38-45. How does the sign of Jonah relate to Jesus' message to the pharisees in verses 37-54?

A – What did the pharisees need to do? Define the word "repent" and then reflect on an area in your life that repentance may be a next step.

The Whole Story

Reading: Luke 12　　　　Date: _____

Praise: _____
_____

Observations: _____
_____
_____
_____
_____
_____
_____
_____

Key Verse: _____
_____

How can I apply this? _____
_____
_____
_____

Prayer: _____
_____
_____
_____

Who can I share this with? _____

Going Deeper:
O – Summarize in short sentences the core teachings in this reading.
A – Which section of this reading has the most significance today? How should I respond?

Jesus' Earthly Ministry: Year 3

Reading: Jonah 1   Date: _____

Praise: _____

Observations: _____
_____
_____
_____
_____
_____
_____

Key Verse: _____

How can I apply this? _____
_____
_____

Prayer: _____
_____
_____

Who can I share this with? _____

Going Deeper:
O – Write out a summary of the events, focusing on the interaction between Jonah and the Lord - and Jonah and the sailors.
A – Put yourself on the boat with one of the sailors – would you have been in favor of throwing Jonah overboard? Why or why not?

The Whole Story

Reading: Jonah 2   Date: _____

Praise: _____
_____

Observations: _____
_____
_____
_____
_____
_____
_____
_____

Key Verse: _____
_____

How can I apply this? _____
_____
_____
_____

Prayer: _____
_____
_____
_____

Who can I share this with? _____

Going Deeper:
O – What did the Lord provide to Jonah? What was Jonah's response?
Apply – Jonah responded with promises of praise from within a very difficult place. Reflect on a time where you were in a difficult place and needed to praise the Lord.

Jesus' Earthly Ministry: Year 3

Reading: Jonah 3 & 4   Date: _____

Praise: _____

_____

Observations: _____

_____
_____
_____
_____
_____
_____
_____

Key Verse: _____

_____

How can I apply this? _____

_____
_____
_____

Prayer: _____

_____
_____
_____

Who can I share this with? _____

Going Deeper:

O – Jonah obeyed the Lord and went to Nineveh, but the Lord relented from the punishment He had Jonah warn them about because of their reactions. What was Jonah's response when the Lord relented? Why?

A – When, if ever, have you been angry with the Lord. Why? Has there been a resolution?

The Whole Story

Message Notes

Date:_____

Jesus' Earthly Ministry: Year 3

Message Notes

The Whole Story

Community Group Notes   Date:_____

Jesus' Earthly Ministry: Year 3

Community Group Notes

The Whole Story

Reading: John 14   Date: _____

Praise: _____

_____

Observations: _____

_____
_____
_____
_____
_____
_____
_____

Key Verse: _____

_____

How can I apply this? _____

_____
_____
_____

Prayer: _____

_____
_____
_____

Who can I share this with? _____

Going Deeper:
O – Make notes on everything Jesus taught about the advocate. By what other name(s) is He called?
A – Which verse in this chapter creates the most hope for you today? Write it out and pray it back to the Lord.

Jesus' Earthly Ministry: Year 3

Reading: John 15   Date: _____

Praise: _____

_____

Observations: _____

_____
_____
_____
_____
_____
_____
_____

Key Verse: _____

_____

How can I apply this? _____

_____
_____
_____

Prayer: _____

_____
_____
_____

Who can I share this with? _____

Going Deeper:
O – "Remain in _____, _____, _____." What is Jesus telling the disciples to do? To whom is the advocate coming from? For Whom?
A – Verse 27 can bring comfort in trying times. Respond.

The Whole Story

Reading: John 16   Date: _____

Praise: _____
_____

Observations: _____
_____
_____
_____
_____
_____
_____
_____

Key Verse: _____
_____

How can I apply this? _____
_____
_____
_____

Prayer: _____
_____
_____
_____

Who can I share this with? _____

Going Deeper:
O – What will the advocate do? What other names does Jesus use to describe Him?
A – In verse 1, Jesus explains why He told the disciples "all of this." Having read John 14-16, what stands out the most today? Spend some quiet time pondering what you've read.

Jesus' Earthly Ministry: Year 3

Reading: John 17   Date: _____

Praise: _____

_____

Observations: _____

_____
_____
_____
_____
_____
_____
_____

Key Verse: _____

_____

How can I apply this? _____

_____
_____
_____

Prayer: _____

_____
_____
_____

Who can I share this with? _____

Going Deeper:
O – Jesus prays to His father for all those who believe in Him. Read His prayer in at least one other translation.
A – What brings the most comfort today from Jesus' prayer to His father?

The Whole Story

Reading: Ezekiel 36   Date: _____

Praise: _____
_____

Observations: _____
_____
_____
_____
_____
_____
_____
_____

Key Verse: _____
_____

How can I apply this? _____
_____
_____
_____

Prayer: _____
_____
_____
_____

Who can I share this with? _____

Going Deeper:
O – How will the Lord restore Israel? List the specifics. What does a "new heart" and a "new spirit" mean (verse 26)?
A – The Lord's purpose for restoring Israel is at the end of verse 38. Do you know that He is Lord? How? Explain?

Jesus' Earthly Ministry: Year 3

Reading: Acts 1   Date: _____

Praise: _____

_____

Observations: _____

_____
_____
_____
_____
_____
_____
_____

Key Verse: _____

_____

How can I apply this? _____

_____
_____
_____

Prayer: _____

_____
_____
_____

Who can I share this with? _____

Going Deeper:
O – Why did Jesus tell the disciples to wait in Jerusalem? What was to come? What were they to do afterwards? (verses 4-8)
A – Can you recall a time when you watched in amazement what Jesus was doing around you? Or a time when you looked back and realized He had been there?

The Whole Story

Message Notes   Date:_____

Jesus' Earthly Ministry: Year 3

Message Notes

The Whole Story

Community Group Notes   Date:_____

Jesus' Earthly Ministry: Year 3

Community Group Notes

The Whole Story

Reading: Matthew 10   Date: _____

Praise: _____

_____

Observations: _____

_____

_____

_____

_____

_____

_____

Key Verse: _____

_____

How can I apply this? _____

_____

_____

Prayer: _____

_____

_____

Who can I share this with? _____

Going Deeper:

O – List the specific instructions Jesus gave to His disciples as He sent them out.

A – What does Jesus' command: "Freely you have received; freely give" mean for you this week?

Jesus' Earthly Ministry: Year 3

Reading: Luke 8   Date: _____

Praise: _____

_____

Observations: _____

_____
_____
_____
_____
_____
_____
_____

Key Verse: _____

_____

How can I apply this? _____

_____
_____
_____

Prayer: _____

_____
_____
_____

Who can I share this with? _____

Going Deeper:

O – What specific attributes of Jesus can you list from this chapter?
A – Which of these attributes have you personally experienced? Use these attributes to praise/thank Him for all He is and for all He has been to you.

The Whole Story

Reading: Isaiah 26   Date: _____

Praise: _____
_____

Observations: _____
_____
_____
_____
_____
_____
_____
_____

Key Verse: _____
_____

How can I apply this? _____
_____
_____
_____

Prayer: _____
_____
_____
_____

Who can I share this with? _____

Going Deeper:
O – Isaiah 26 is a song of praise! List 5 things for which the author is praising the Lord.
A – Which verse is most meaningful for you? Why? Memorize it.

Jesus' Earthly Ministry: Year 3

Reading: Ezekiel 37   Date: _____

Praise: _____

_____

Observations: _____

_____

_____

_____

_____

_____

_____

_____

Key Verse: _____

_____

How can I apply this? _____

_____

_____

_____

Prayer: _____

_____

_____

_____

Who can I share this with? _____

Going Deeper:

O – Scan the passages for this week and list verses which reveal the Lord's power over physical life and death.

A – Look at Ezekiel 37:15-28 together with Isaiah 26:19. What do you think will happen to the Church (the completed Israel) at some future time? What difference does this make in the way you live today?

The Whole Story

Reading: Job 19   Date: _____

Praise: _____

_____

Observations: _____

_____

_____

_____

_____

_____

_____

_____

Key Verse: _____

_____

How can I apply this? _____

_____

_____

_____

Prayer: _____

_____

_____

_____

Who can I share this with? _____

Going Deeper:

O – Who was Job addressing in this passage? In one sentence describe Job's frame of mind in verse 24.

A – How does Job's hope expressed in verses 25-27 encourage you today? If you have not already done so, memorize Isaiah 26:19 and Job 19:25-27. Ask the Lord for the opportunity to encourage someone else with what you have learned.

Jesus' Earthly Ministry: Year 3

Reading: John 11   Date: _____

Praise: _____

_____

Observations: _____

_____

_____

_____

_____

_____

_____

_____

Key Verse: _____

How can I apply this? _____

_____

_____

_____

Prayer: _____

_____

_____

_____

Who can I share this with? _____

Going Deeper:
O – List things that surprise you in the account of Lazarus' death and resurrection.
A – In light of everything we have studied this week about death, what is your current attitude toward your own death and the deaths of those you love?

The Whole Story

Message Notes   Date:_____

Jesus' Earthly Ministry: Year 3

Message Notes

The Whole Story

Community Group Notes   Date:_____

Jesus' Earthly Ministry: Year 3

Community Group Notes

The Whole Story

Reading: Matthew 21   Date: _____

Praise: _____
_____

Observations: _____
_____
_____
_____
_____
_____
_____
_____

Key Verse: _____
_____

How can I apply this? _____
_____
_____
_____

Prayer: _____
_____
_____
_____

Who can I share this with? _____

Going Deeper:

O – Make notes about how the people responded to Jesus; how the disciples responded; and how the teachers of the law and chief priests responded.

A – Reflect on which of these groups might you find yourself in the middle of if you might have been in Jerusalem on that day. How might your response have been similar or different?

Jesus' Earthly Ministry: Year 3

Reading: Jeremiah 7   Date: _____

Praise: _____

_____

Observations: _____

_____

_____

_____

_____

_____

_____

_____

_____

Key Verse: _____

_____

How can I apply this? _____

_____

_____

_____

Prayer: _____

_____

_____

_____

Who can I share this with? _____

Going Deeper:

O – In Matthew 21 we read about Jesus clearing the temple. What is there in Jeremiah 7 that shows us this isn't the first time the Israelites have had issues with the temple? What is similar in the two accounts? What is different?

A – Reflect on your worship, prayer, and Bible study time. Are there things that get in the way between you and the Lord? Explain.

The Whole Story

Reading: Luke 19   Date: _____

Praise: _____
_____

Observations: _____
_____
_____
_____
_____
_____
_____
_____

Key Verse: _____
_____

How can I apply this? _____
_____
_____
_____

Prayer: _____
_____
_____
_____

Who can I share this with? _____

Going Deeper:
O – Jesus came to Jerusalem as a King. We read this in Matthew 21, as well. List what happened in both tellings of the event and what made this so special.
A – The people threw their coats on the ground so the donkey would walk on them. How might a crowd show honor to Jesus if he came into your town today? How might you react?

Jesus' Earthly Ministry: Year 3

Reading: Jeremiah 11   Date: _____

Praise: _____

Observations: _____

_____
_____
_____
_____
_____
_____
_____

Key Verse: _____

_____

How can I apply this? _____

_____
_____
_____

Prayer: _____

_____
_____
_____

Who can I share this with? _____

Going Deeper:
O – "Obey me and do everything I command you, and you will be my people, and I will be your God." (verse 4). What did the Lord want from Israel?
A – Reflect on that verse in your own life.

The Whole Story

Reading: Isaiah 56   Date: _____

Praise: _____
_____

Observations: _____
_____
_____
_____
_____
_____
_____
_____

Key Verse: _____
_____

How can I apply this? _____
_____
_____
_____

Prayer: _____
_____
_____
_____

Who can I share this with? _____

Going Deeper:
O – The phrase "who keeps the Sabbath" is repeated several times. What is the Lord asking, specifically?
A – How is that phrase connected to verse 7 "I will… give them joy in my house of prayer?" How do either of them apply to you today?

Jesus' Earthly Ministry: Year 3

Reading: Haggai 2   Date: _____

Praise: _____

Observations: _____

_____
_____
_____
_____
_____
_____

Key Verse: _____

_____

How can I apply this? _____

_____
_____
_____

Prayer: _____

_____
_____
_____

Who can I share this with? _____

Going Deeper:

O – The Lord made a declaration to His people about the temple that was to be rebuilt in Jerusalem. What did he say?
A – The Lord said he would grant peace in the new temple. Did Jesus find peace in the temple in Jerusalem? (See also John 2). Does the temple relate to anything within each of us today? How?

The Whole Story

Message Notes

Date:_____

Jesus' Earthly Ministry: Year 3

Message Notes

The Whole Story

Community Group Notes   Date:_____

Jesus' Earthly Ministry: Year 3

Community Group Notes

The Whole Story

Reading: Mark 12   Date: _____

Praise: _____
_____

Observations: _____
_____
_____
_____
_____
_____
_____
_____

Key Verse: _____
_____

How can I apply this? _____
_____
_____
_____

Prayer: _____
_____
_____
_____

Who can I share this with? _____

Going Deeper:
O – This chapter has 7 separate sections. Write down each section heading and a one-line summary of each parable attached to it.
A – Which of these parables stands out to you today? Why?

Jesus' Earthly Ministry: Year 3

Reading: Luke 16   Date: _____

Praise: _____

_____

Observations: _____

_____
_____
_____
_____
_____
_____
_____

Key Verse: _____

_____

How can I apply this? _____

_____
_____
_____

Prayer: _____

_____
_____
_____

Who can I share this with? _____

Going Deeper:

O – *Two key verses in this chapter are in verse 13 and verse 31. Choose one and explain how it relates to the parable it is contained within.*

A – *Why did you pick the verse above? What about it resonates with you? Explain.*

The Whole Story

Reading: Malachi 3   Date: _____

Praise: _____
_____

Observations: _____
_____
_____
_____
_____
_____
_____
_____

Key Verse: _____
_____

How can I apply this? _____
_____
_____
_____

Prayer: _____
_____
_____
_____

Who can I share this with? _____

Going Deeper:
O – Tithing. What does the Lord teach Israel about tithing through Malachi the prophet? Summarize the story of the widow's offering in Mark 12:41-44. How are these two passages related?
A – Spend some quiet time reflecting on what you read today and make some notes about your response.

Jesus' Earthly Ministry: Year 3

Reading: Luke 20   Date: _____

Praise: _____

_____

Observations: _____

_____

_____

_____

_____

_____

_____

Key Verse: _____

_____

How can I apply this? _____

_____

_____

Prayer: _____

_____

_____

_____

Who can I share this with? _____

Going Deeper:
O – Paying Taxes to Caesar. We read this in Mark 12 earlier this week. What does Jesus say about the Roman coins? Why is He telling this story? Who is the audience? What do they want?
A – What does Jesus say in verses 45-47? Reflect.

The Whole Story

Reading: Luke 21   Date: _____

Praise: _____

_____

Observations: _____

_____

_____

_____

_____

_____

_____

_____

Key Verse: _____

_____

How can I apply this? _____

_____

_____

_____

Prayer: _____

_____

_____

_____

Who can I share this with? _____

Going Deeper:

O – Who was coming to listen to Jesus teach at the temple every day? (verses 37-38). Outline His teaching in this chapter. Does anything stand out? What?

A – Reflect on what you noted that stood out in this chapter. Why did you choose it?

Jesus' Earthly Ministry: Year 3

Reading: Matthew 26   Date: _____

Praise: _____

_____

Observations: _____

_____
_____
_____
_____
_____
_____
_____

Key Verse: _____

_____

How can I apply this? _____

_____
_____
_____

Prayer: _____

_____
_____
_____

Who can I share this with? _____

Going Deeper:
O – Read through this chapter several times and in at least two different translations of the Bible.
A – Take time to quietly ponder what you read. Summarize the entire chapter in 5 words or less. Reflect on the words that you chose.

The Whole Story

Message Notes   Date:_____

Jesus' Earthly Ministry: Year 3

Message Notes

The Whole Story

Community Group Notes   Date:_____

Jesus' Earthly Ministry: Year 3

Community Group Notes

The Whole Story

The Cross

Weeks Nineteen and Twenty

The Whole Story

Including Your Entire Family in The Whole Story:

The Cross

Big Truth
Jesus died for you because he loves you.

Sing
Jesus Paid It All

Pray
Have mercy on me, O God,
   according to your unfailing love;
according to your great compassion
   blot out my transgressions.
Wash away all my iniquity
   and cleanse me from my sin.

For I know my transgressions,
   and my sin is always before me.
Against you, you only, have I sinned
   and done what is evil in your sight;
so you are right in your verdict
   and justified when you judge.   Psalm 51:1-4

Read and Talk About
John 19:16 - 20:8

Memorize
Now this is eternal life: that they know you, the only true God, and Jesus Christ, whom you have sent.   John 17:3

Activity
Share about your faith or about what you are learning with God with someone you know. Talk as a family about who you might be able to talk to and follow up with each other as the month goes on. Even young children can participate in talking to their friends.

The Whole Story

Reading: Mark 11 & 14   Date: _____

Praise: _____
_____

Observations: _____
_____
_____
_____
_____
_____
_____
_____

Key Verse: _____
_____

How can I apply this? _____
_____
_____
_____

Prayer: _____
_____
_____
_____

Who can I share this with? _____

Going Deeper:
O – Mark 11 is a review of Jesus' arrival in Jerusalem. Is there anything new that you read in this gospel? Mark 14 tells the story of the last supper and Jesus' arrest. Write a brief summary of the events.
A – Reflect on the events in Mark 14.

The Cross

Reading: Luke 22   Date: _____

Praise: _____

_____

Observations: _____

_____

_____

_____

_____

_____

_____

_____

Key Verse: _____

_____

How can I apply this? _____

_____

_____

Prayer: _____

_____

_____

Who can I share this with? _____

Going Deeper:
O – Write out a brief summary of the events. Compare your notes to those you wrote yesterday and from Matthew 26.
A – Spend some quiet time reflecting on these events.

The Whole Story

Reading: Luke 23   Date: _____

Praise: _____
_____

Observations: _____
_____
_____
_____
_____
_____
_____
_____

Key Verse: _____
_____

How can I apply this? _____
_____
_____
_____

Prayer: _____
_____
_____
_____

Who can I share this with? _____

Going Deeper:
O – Jesus is crucified, dies and is buried. Make notes on what happened. Who/What/Where/Why/When/How.
A – Spend at least 15-30 minutes reading and re-reading this chapter. Quietly reflect.

The Cross

Reading: John 18   Date: _____

Praise: _____

Observations: _____
_____
_____
_____
_____
_____
_____
_____

Key Verse: _____

How can I apply this? _____
_____
_____

Prayer: _____
_____
_____

Who can I share this with? _____

Going Deeper:
O – Peter, Peter, Peter. What did Peter say and do?
A – Reflect on Jesus' response to Pilate in verse 37. How does it apply to you?

The Whole Story

Reading: John 19   Date: _____

Praise: _____
_____

Observations: _____
_____
_____
_____
_____
_____
_____
_____

Key Verse: _____
_____

How can I apply this? _____
_____
_____
_____

Prayer: _____
_____
_____
_____

Who can I share this with? _____

Going Deeper:
O – Make notes on what happened.
Who/What/Where/Why/When/How. Compare it to you notes on Luke 23.
A – Choose at least one other translation to read this chapter in. Spend quiet time reflecting on all that happened.

The Cross

Reading: Matthew 27   Date: _____

Praise: _____

_____

Observations: _____

_____

_____

_____

_____

_____

_____

_____

Key Verse: _____

_____

How can I apply this? _____

_____

_____

_____

Prayer: _____

_____

_____

_____

Who can I share this with? _____

Going Deeper:

O – What is different in this gospel's writing about the crucifixion, death and burial of Jesus? How does it affect your understanding of the events?

Apply – As we prepare for worship tomorrow, reflect on what you have read this week. How might your life be different next week after having reflected on these events during this week?

The Whole Story

Message Notes   Date:_____

The Cross

Message Notes

The Whole Story

Community Group Notes   Date:_____

The Cross

Community Group Notes

The Whole Story

Reading: Mark 15   Date: _____

Praise: _____
_____

Observations: _____
_____
_____
_____
_____
_____
_____
_____

Key Verse: _____
_____

How can I apply this? _____
_____
_____
_____

Prayer: _____
_____
_____
_____

Who can I share this with? _____

Going Deeper:
O – The last of the four gospel writings about the crucifixion, death and burial of Jesus is in the book of Mark. What is added or left out of his account?
A – Reflect back on all of the events that happened from the time of Jesus' triumphal entry into Jerusalem until his burial. What stands out the most to you? Why?

The Cross

Reading: Mark 16   Date: _____

Praise: _____

_____

Observations: _____

_____
_____
_____
_____
_____
_____
_____

Key Verse: _____

_____

How can I apply this? _____

_____
_____
_____

Prayer: _____

_____
_____
_____

Who can I share this with? _____

Going Deeper:
O – JESUS HAS RISEN!!!! Summarize what happened.
A – React and reflect with a time of worship and celebration!

The Whole Story

Reading: Luke 24   Date: _____

Praise: _____

_____

Observations: _____

_____
_____
_____
_____
_____
_____
_____
_____

Key Verse: _____

_____

How can I apply this? _____

_____
_____
_____

Prayer: _____

_____
_____
_____

Who can I share this with? _____

Going Deeper:
O – JESUS HAS RISEN!!!!! Summarize what Luke wrote and what Jesus said.
A – How did the disciples react? What surprises you about their reaction?

The Cross

Reading: Matthew 28   Date: _____

Praise: _____
_____

Observations: _____
_____
_____
_____
_____
_____
_____
_____
_____

Key Verse: _____

How can I apply this? _____
_____
_____
_____

Prayer: _____
_____
_____
_____

Who can I share this with? _____

Going Deeper:
O – JESUS HAS RISEN!!!!! Summarize the details that Matthew wrote. What happened with the guards? Why?
A – "But some doubted" (verse 17). Do you have any doubts about what we've read in the last two weeks? Share them with the Lord in prayer.

The Whole Story

Reading: John 20 & 21   Date: _____

Praise: _____
_____

Observations: _____
_____
_____
_____
_____
_____
_____
_____

Key Verse: _____
_____

How can I apply this? _____
_____
_____
_____

Prayer: _____
_____
_____
_____

Who can I share this with? _____

Going Deeper:
O – THE TOMB IS EMPTY!!!!! Who did Jesus appear to? Summarize.
A – Celebrate this great news in prayer, worship and song.

The Cross

Reading: 1 Corinthians 15   Date: _____

Praise: _____

_____

Observations: _____

_____
_____
_____
_____
_____
_____
_____

Key Verse: _____

_____

How can I apply this? _____

_____
_____
_____

Prayer: _____

_____
_____
_____

Who can I share this with? _____

Going Deeper:
O – How does Paul recount the story of Christ's death, burial and resurrection?
A – Write out to memorize verses 3-8. What do these verses mean to you?

The Whole Story

Message Notes   Date:_____

Message Notes

The Whole Story

Community Group Notes   Date:_____

The Cross

Community Group Notes

The Whole Story

Going Deeper

Here are some suggestions on how to "Go Deeper" using the daily pages.

Stay Silent:

One option for growing deeper in your relationship with the Lord is to spend dedicated times of silence just listening for God speaking to you. Try writing down how many minutes that day you were silent. This isn't time to tell the Lord what you want to say, or to sing along with a worship song. It's time in stillness and quiet, listening and waiting for the Lord to answer or guide you. This time often happens naturally between the *Observation* and the *Application* sections of the daily journal. If this is a new discipline for you, try starting every day for the first week with one minute of silence. Add a minute each week. Three to four minutes of silence and stillness is often more than we are accustomed to but can be an important time of tuning out our own voice and listening for God. On each daily guide page you can simply write down the number of minutes you were silent that day.

Prayers:

When you pray for someone, for a situation, or for wisdom – make a note of the date and your prayer. Review your list often as a reminder of how the Lord is working. Write down the date that any of your prayers are answered as a milestone to look back and reflect on. Pages for recording prayers begin on page 224.

The Whole Story

Commit it to Memory:

A memory verse is any verse or verses in the Bible that you want to know by heart. Writing the verse(s) out every day until you have them memorized can help to bury the verse deeper into your memory. There's no right amount of time it should take you to memorize a verse. Some will come to memory so quickly that by the end of a week you'll have it down. Others may take longer. Sometimes they jump out of a Scripture passage that you're reading as something that is comforting or challenging. Sometimes the pastor will include a verse in a message that you want to remember. Maybe you have a daily Bible verse app that sends a verse daily. Wherever you find a verse, write it every day in the *Going Deeper* section of the guide until you have it mastered, then record at the end in the *Memory Verses* section. Once you've got one done, it's time to start a new one! Write down the date that you memorized the verse so that you will have a record to look back on.

Including Your Entire Family in The Whole Story:

Spending quiet time with God is a blessing. It is a gift that you are offering your family. If spending personal quiet time has not been a part of your family culture, give yourself grace and time to build habits of faith in your family. Charlotte Mason said, "The habits of the child produce the character of the man." Teach them to build a habit of reading and loving the Word of God. Choose one or two ideas from this list to get started building habits of faith. Here are some ideas for including your whole family in the Whole Story series:

1. Include your children in the daily readings. It is so important that your children are hearing the Word of God as it is written. Show your children that the Bible is a source of wisdom, joy, and love. Read it to them or listen to the reading on the Trinity Church App while you're in the car or getting ready for your day.

Going Deeper

2. Pray for your kids. Pray with your kids. Let your kids pray alone and with you. The Holy Spirit can and will speak to your children, and not just through you.
3. Discuss the reading at a consistent time every day, for example over breakfast. Ask your children consistent questions about the reading – What happened? Where do we see God's love for His people in these verses?
4. Share what you are learning with them. It will hold you accountable, reinforce what you are learning, and create a common vocabulary. Be honest when Scripture is hard to understand or when you miss a day of Scripture reading.
5. Memorize Scripture together. Keep a card on the breakfast table and have someone read it each day. You can print the suggested Scripture Memory Cards from The Whole Story webpage – TrinityChurchVB.com/thewholestory.

Family Scripture Celebrations:

As you go through the devotional, you will see a monthly Family Scripture Celebration at the beginning of each theme we study. Set an appointment on your calendar to spend some time in the word together. Even 15 minutes will set a tone for your family.

Each Celebration includes a hymn, a verse to memorize for the month, a scripture to pray, a scripture to read, and an activity. We have created a Spotify playlist with all the monthly hymns that you can find at TrinityChurchVB.com/TheWholeStory.

We created these family times for people with no kids, young kids, and older kids. We hope that these guided and intentional times are something you look forward to doing as a family.

Additional Resources:

Here are some additional resources to help you create a family culture of faith:

https://www.notconsumed.com/secrets-to-cultivating-kids-devotional-habits/

https://www.focusonthefamily.com/topic/parenting/teaching-faith-to-kids/

https://wholeheart.org/family-faith-project

Community Group:

Community Groups are a key way you can get connected with a group of people who are following Jesus together – whether at a Trinity Church campus or around the world. Find a diverse group of people whom you may not have connected with otherwise and commit to meeting together at least every other week to share what you are learning in the Bible and to support each other through prayer and other practical ways. You'll find that we are all living out our faith in differently and we have plenty to learn from each other. If you are not near a Trinity Church campus, check out churches in your area and explore joining a group nearby. You can also start your own group by inviting a few friends over for coffee or tea and sharing together what you have learned from one chapter of your Bible reading that week. Pages for community group notes are included with each week after the message notes pages.

An additional guide to use with a group can be found in the community groups section at:
https://www.TrinityChurchVB.com/TheWholeStory

To find a group meeting near a Trinity Church campus, go to:
http://www.TrinityChurchVB.com/groups

Going Deeper

Prayers

Date Added	Date Answered	

The Whole Story

Prayers

Date Added	Date Answered	

Going Deeper

Prayers

Date Added	Date Answered	

The Whole Story

Prayers

Date Added	Date Answered	

Going Deeper

Prayers

Date Added	Date Answered	

The Whole Story

Prayers

Date Added	Date Answered	

Going Deeper

Prayers

Date Added	Date Answered	

The Whole Story

Prayers

Date Added	Date Answered	

Going Deeper

Memory Verses

The Whole Story

Memory Verses

Going Deeper

Memory Verses

The Whole Story

Memory Verses

Who We Are

Separated from God

The Bible tells us that when God created everything, it was all good. But Adam and Eve chose their own way instead of God's way. That's a choice that all humanity makes, and it's called sin. Sin separates us from God because he's perfect.

"Light has come into the world, but men loved darkness instead of light." John 3:19

How can you bridge the gap between a perfect God and imperfect people?

The Only Way to God

At creation, God created humans to have a relationship with him. He loves you and has a desire to have a personal relationship with you. Though sin separates you from God, he has provided a solution in the person of Jesus Christ. He accepted the punishment for your sin by dying on the cross. Then Jesus defeated sin to provide a hope for your future by rising from the dead and provided a way to have eternal life with God. **"For God so loved the world that he gave his one and only Son, that whoever believes in him shall not perish but have eternal life." John 3:16**

"But God demonstrates his own love for us in this: that while we were still sinners, Christ died for us." Romans 5:8

The Whole Story

Jesus became the way for you to have a relationship with God the Father. **"I am the way and the truth and the life. No one comes to the Father except through me." John 14:6**

How to Choose Jesus

1. Admit that you are a sinner and turn away from sin. (See John 8:11)
2. Believe (have faith) that Jesus died on the cross for your sin and rose from death to give you abundant life on earth and eternal life after death. (See Romans 10:9)
3. Receive Jesus and ask (pray for) him to come in and control your life through the Holy Spirit (receive him as your Lord and Savior)

A Sample Prayer

Here is a suggested prayer that you can use if you'd like to accept Jesus as your Lord and Savior. The exact wording isn't what matters, but rather the attitude of your heart:

"Lord Jesus, thank you for showing me my need for you. Thank you for dying on the cross for me and for promising me an abundant life and life eternal. Please forgive all my sins and failures. Make me clean and help me start fresh with You. I want to trust Jesus as my Savior and follow him as Lord for the rest of my life. Help me to love and to serve You with all my heart. Amen."

What Next

Becoming a Christian is just the first step of a lifetime journey toward knowing God. You now have a personal relationship with God your Father, and there are some steps you can take to deepen that relationship. Here are some ideas to make each day a day that honors God and helps you to grow in faith:

Who We Are

- Tell someone who is already a Christian about your decision-maybe a friend, a pastor or a co-worker
- Read a part of the Bible each day
- Pray each day, talking to God like you would to someone you know
- Join a church where the Bible is taught

The Whole Story

ABOUT TRINITY CHURCH

Mission: Trinity Church exists to make disciples who exalt Jesus Christ and honor God's Word in all that they say and do.

Vision: By God's Spirit, Trinity Church will be a multisite church without walls reaching people with the Gospel in Hampton Roads, Virginia and the four corners of the earth. We will make disciples not just converts, have a kingdom mindset, pray about everything, value each person's calling and worship God through the glory of the old and the promise of the new.

Strategy: We will help people COME to faith in Jesus Christ, GROW as his disciples, SERVE as Jesus served and REACH those who do not yet know him.

A Church without Walls: We are a church without walls not because we don't own a building (that is one reason but not the only one). We are a church without walls because the church of God is simply the people of God and we are without walls because it is our job to live like the people of God outside the walls where we worship. It is our unique calling—every one of us, not just those who are leaders in the church—to take this glorious Gospel to every part of the world where we work, live and interact.

TrinityChurchVB.com

Made in the USA
Lexington, KY
29 October 2019